Aberdeenshire's Lost Railw

by
Gordon Stansfield

A railtour special visiting the closed station at Alford, June 1960.

ACKNOWLEDGEMENTS
The publishers wish to thank the following for contributing the pictures in
this book: Hugh Brodie for the front cover, pages 5, 6, 7, 8, 9, 10, 11, 12, 13,
15, 16, 17, 18, 19, 20, 23, 26, 27, 29, 30, 31, 32, 34, 37, 41, 42, 43, 44 and the
inside back cover; the Rex Conway Steam Collection for pages 2, 3, 21, 22,
24, 25, 36 and 39; Rev. D.J. Lane for page 35 and both images on page 48;
Neville Stead for page 47 and the back cover; Neville Stead/D. Butterfield
for pages 1 and 4; Neville Stead/P.B. Booth for page 40; Stations UK for
pages 28, 33 and 46.

The shed at Boddam Station.

INTRODUCTION

At the beginning of the twentieth century most small towns and villages within the county of Aberdeenshire could be reached by rail. From Aberdeen's imposing Joint Station passengers could travel far and wide and branch lines stretched in every direction. Westwards, the Deeside line ran to Ballater and on this royal trains frequently ran, carrying Queen Victoria to Balmoral. Northwards, the towns of Fraserburgh and Peterhead also had rail links along with some of the smaller coastal villages such as St Combs and Boddam. Northwest from Aberdeen, on the present day line from Aberdeen to Inverness, branch lines panned out to Alford, Old Meldrum and Macduff. Today, these lines are just a memory.

The establishment of the railways from the 1860s onwards brought opportunity and prosperity to the county. Fish traffic from ports such as Fraserburgh could be moved cheaply and efficiently to new markets south of the border and farmers also made good use of the railway to move their produce and livestock. Even Aberdeenshire's famous granite could now be transported easily by rail from quarries at Kemnay to locations all over the country.

To the ordinary working person the railways opened up new horizons. The main operator in the county up until 1923 was the Great North of Scotland Railway who ran not only scheduled services, but also cheap excursions to places of interest like the geological formations at Bullers O'Buchan and their special platform for pilgrimages to New Deer Abbey. Trips to destinations further afield such as the Spey Valley were also popular. Sunday train services didn't really begin until the late 1920s but soon gave way to the new bus services which, along with the emergence of the motor car, caused the gradual shrinkage of the county's rail network.

Following the Railway Act of 1921, which created four large companies for the whole of Britain, the Great North of Scotland was succeeded in 1923 by the London and North Eastern Railway who operated services until Britain's railways were nationalised in 1948.

Today rail journeys in Aberdeenshire are predominantly long distance although up until 1937 suburban services operated in and around Aberdeen. Known to Aberdonians as 'the subbies' these services, running to Dyce, started in 1887 and were known as the Jubilee trains. There was also the service between Aberdeen and Culter on the Deeside line. These, and many other services, are long gone but it is hoped that this book will rekindle memories of Aberdeenshire's bygone railways and serve as a reminder of just how important they were to thousands of people all over the county.

Philorth Bridge Halt.

Aberdeen: Guild Street – Goods Branch Junction

Passenger service withdrawn	4 November 1867	*Station closed*	*Date*
Distance	0.5 miles	Guild Street	4 November 1867
Company	Aberdeen Railway Company		

Guild Street Station, opened in August 1854, was the city terminus of the Aberdeen Railway Company and the forerunner of the Joint Station that the company ran with the Great North of Scotland Railway which is still in use today. The station was adjacent to the harbour area and passengers heading north towards Elgin were required to travel by a horse drawn coach to the Great North of Scotland terminus at Waterloo. With the opening of the Joint Station the need for a passenger station ended although the line continued in use for freight.

A railtour special at Aberdeen Waterloo, June 1960. After closure to passenger services, the station remained in use as a goods station.

Aberdeen: Waterloo – Kittybrewster

Passenger service withdrawn	4 November 1867	*Station closed*	*Date*
Distance	1.75 miles	Waterloo	4 November 1867
Company	Great North of Scotland		

This line opened for freight traffic in September 1855 and a passenger service was introduced the following April, although the need for this ceased when the Joint Station was opened on 4 November 1867. Known as Aberdeen Joint Station until 1952 (when its name was changed to Aberdeen), this was owned by the Aberdeen Joint Station Committee and provided the city with a major terminal station allowing trains through from the south to the north. There were three through platforms in addition to four terminal bays. In 1869 this facility enabled the operation of the longest through coach working in Britain when coaches on the daily mail train from London Euston to Aberdeen were extended to run to Elgin – a distance of 620 miles with a journey time of 22 hours.

Alford – Kintore (Kintore Junction)

Passenger service withdrawn	2 January 1950	*Stations closed*	*Date*
Distance	16 miles	Tillyfourie	2 January 1950
Company	Great North of Scotland	Monymusk	2 January 1950
		Kemnay	2 January 1950
Stations closed	*Date*	Ratchhill Siding *	After 1938
Alford	2 January 1950	Paradise Siding *	After 1938
Whitehouse	2 January 1950		

Monymusk Station, *c.* **1906.**

* Used by workmen only.

Kemnay Station was demolished in April 1967.

Alford was a branch line terminus which opened to passenger traffic on 21 March 1859 and the branch left the Great North of Scotland's Aberdeen to Elgin line at Kintore. It took three years to build and was originally owned by the Alford Valley Railway before it amalgamated with the Great North of Scotland system in 1866.

The line enabled the granite quarry industry at Kemnay and Tillyfourie to expand and as a result there was a large amount of freight traffic. Kemnay was just a hamlet when the railway arrived but by 1901 its population had risen to over 1,000 due to the quarry workings which supplied granite for London's kerb and paving stones, amongst other uses. The pattern of passenger services was about average for such a branch line with four return journeys each weekday. In the year prior to closure the number of return journeys was down to three with the average sixteen mile journey taking about forty minutes. The junction station at Kintore closed to passengers on 7 December 1964 although freight services along the line lasted for another two years.

Ballater – Aberdeen (Ferryhill Junction)

Passenger service withdrawn	28 February 1966
Distance	42.75 miles
Company	Great North of Scotland

Stations closed	*Date*
Ballater	28 February 1966
Cambus O'May	28 February 1966
Dinnet	28 February 1966
Aboyne	28 February 1966
Aboyne Curling Pond Platform *	Not known
Dess	28 February 1966
Lumphanan	28 February 1966
Torphins	28 February 1966
Craigmyle Siding **	By June 1911
Glassel	28 February 1966
Dee Street Halt	28 February 1966
Banchory (first) (Kincardineshire)	2 December 1859
Banchory (second)	1902

Stations closed	*Date*
Banchory (third)	28 February 1966
Crathes Castle Halt (Kincardineshire)	1 January 1863
Crathes (Kincardineshire)	28 February 1966
Mills of Drum	1 January 1863
Park	28 February 1966
Drum	10 September 1951
Culter	28 February 1966
Milltimber	5 April 1937
Murtle	5 April 1937
Bieldside	5 April 1937
West Cults	5 April 1937
Cults (first)	1855
Cults (second)	28 February 1966
Pitfodels Halt ***	5 April 1937
Ruthrieston ****	5 April 1937
Holburn Street	5 April 1937

* Also known as Loch of Aboyne Platform and
  Curlers' Platform.
** Private station.
*** Known as Pitfodels until July 1926.
**** Closed from April 1876 to June 1885.

Edward VII on his way to Balmoral, *c*. 1906.

Known as the Deeside Railway, the first part of this line opened between Aberdeen and Banchory in 1853. An extension to Aboyne was opened in December 1859 and the last stage to Ballater was in use by October 1866. There were plans to extend the line further and to this end earth works were completed as far as Bridge of Gairn but the idea fell through. The Deeside was famous for its royal trains which carried the Royal Family to Ballater for their holidays at Balmoral Castle. In addition to these there were special Messenger Trains for urgent despatches from London. Services on the line also varied from express trains stopping at only a few stations to short workings from Banchory and Culter which stopped at all intermediate stations. In the 1950s, when British Railways was running the services, attempts were made to keep running costs down. A two coach battery railcar service was introduced in 1958 and the railcars were charged overnight at Aberdeen and Ballater stations using electricity supplied by the North of Scotland Hydro Electric Board. Passenger services were completely withdrawn in 1966 with freight services suffering the same fate shortly afterwards.

Aboyne Station.

Lumphanan Station, *c.* 1920.

Park Station.

Culter Station, *c.* **1907.**

Murtle Station.

King Edward and Queen Alexandra on a visit to Aberdeen in 1903.

Boddam – Ellon (Ellon Junction)

Passenger service withdrawn	31 October 1932	*Stations closed*	*Date*
Distance	15.50 miles	Bullers O'Buchan Halt	31 October 1932
Company	Great North of Scotland	Cruden Bay	31 October 1932
		Hatton	31 October 1932
Stations closed	*Date*	Pitlurg	31 October 1932
Boddam	31 October 1932	Auchmacoy	31 October 1932
Longhaven	31 October 1932		

Cruden Bay Station, *c.* 1905.

HATTON FROM STATION.

Authorised in August 1893, this line opened four years later and was known as the Cruden Railway. The whole length of the route was single track and all the stations were opened on the same date as the line itself. In 1900 a halt was opened at Bullers O'Buchan for people who wished to visit a series of natural geographical cauldrons which had been discovered among the cliffs in the area and in 1899 the company opened a luxury hotel in Cruden Bay. To transport both passengers and goods, an electric tramway system was installed to cover the one mile between the local station and the hotel. The railway line was never really a success as the hotel was not profitable and the fish traffic from Boddam failed to reach anticipated levels. The distance from Boddam to Peterhead was just three miles and if Peterhead had been reached by rail from Boddam the line might have lasted much longer. During the Second World War the Cruden Bay Hotel was requisitioned by the army and it was demolished between 1947 and 1952. The line between Ellon and Cruden Bay was used by troop trains during 1940 and 1941 and freight services were discontinued in November 1945.

Fraserburgh – Dyce (Dyce Junction)

		Stations closed	Date
Passenger service withdrawn	4 October 1965	Brucklay	4 October 1965
Distance	41 miles	Maud **	4 October 1965
Company	Great North of Scotland	Auchnagatt	4 October 1965
		Arnage	4 October 1965
Stations closed	Date	Ellon ***	4 October 1965
Fraserburgh	4 October 1965	Esslemont	15 September 1952
Philorth Halt	4 October 1965	Logierieve	4 October 1965
Rathen	4 October 1965	Udny	4 October 1965
Lonmay	4 October 1965	Newmachar	4 October 1965
Mormond Halt *	4 October 1965	Parkhill	3 April 1950
Strichen	4 October 1965		

Fraserburgh Station, 1906.

* Known as Mormond until June 1939.

** Known as Maud Junction until September 1925.
*** Known as Ellon For Cruden Bay until August 1897.

Philorth Halt.

Known as the Buchan Line, this route linked Fraserburgh with Aberdeen. Several branches radiated from the line: at Ellon there was the branch line to Cruden Bay and Boddam; at Maud Junction the branch line to Peterhead; and at Fraserburgh the light railway to St Combs. Opened in stages and completed in April 1865, the line carried a large amount of fishing traffic as there was a large fishing fleet based in Fraserburgh. The journey time for the line was rather slow with the forty five mile trip to Aberdeen taking an hour and three quarters. Philorth Halt was a station built for the use of a local landowner, Lord Saltoun, who ensured that the Great North of Scotland complied with his condition that the line could cross his land only as long as any member of his family could stop any passenger or goods train whenever they wanted on or off. Another feature of the journey was near Mormond Halt at Mormond Hill where passengers could see the figures of a white horse and stag which had been cut out in the turf in the eighteenth century. Taking up nearly half an acre, the figures can still be seen today. Freight traffic continued along the line to Fraserburgh until 1979 including oil pipe trains which began arriving at Maud in June 1976.

Rathen Station.

Snowdrifts like this were by no means uncommon at Lonmay.

Lonmay Station.

Strichen Station.

Brucklay Station, 1953.

The Station, Maud

Ellon Station, *c.* 1906.

Lenabo – Longside

Passenger service withdrawn	1920
Distance	2.5 miles
Company	Great North of Scotland

Station closed	*Date*
Lenabo	1920

Lenabo Airship Station was built by the Royal Naval Air Service during the First World War, a time when they used a large number of airships. It was reached by a short branch line from Longside Station on the branch between Peterhead and Maud Junction. Leaving Longside, the line crossed some minor roads before reaching the perimeter fence of the airship station. It then continued for a short distance before terminating inside the airship area. By 1923 the rail lines had all been removed and it is probable that during the line's operational days passenger traffic was carried such as the station's personnel. Some remains of the airship station can still be found in the forest which now surrounds this area.

Macduff – Inveramsay (Inveramsay Junction) *

Passenger service withdrawn	1 October 1951		
Distance	29.75 miles		
Company	Great North of Scotland		

Stations Closed	*Date*	*Stations Closed*	*Date*
King Edward	1 October 1951	Turriff	1 October 1951
Plaidy	22 May 1944	Auchterless	1 October 1951
		Fyvie	1 October 1951
		Rothie-Norman	1 October 1951
		Wartle	1 October 1951

Turriff Station.

* The closed stations on this line that were in Banffshire were Banff and Macduff (first), Macduff, and Banff Bridge.

This branch line left the present day Inverness to Aberdeen route at Inveramsay Junction where a station was built to accommodate the new traffic on the line. Opened as far as Turriff in 1857, the line was not extended to Macduff until 1871. The line was closed completely from Macduff to Turriff in 1961 and from Turriff to Inveramsay in January 1966.

Wartle Station.

Murcar Golf Club – Bridge of Don

Passenger service withdrawn	1949	*Stations closed*	*Date*
Distance	2 miles	Murcar Golf Club	1949
Company	Strabathie Light Railway	Bridge of Don	1949

Opened in 1899, this was a three feet narrow gauge railway which was known as the Strabathie Light Railway. It ran from Bridge of Don just outside Aberdeen to the premises of the Seaton Brick and Tile Company's Blackdog Brickworks. Although bricks were carried, a passenger service was operated using, at one time, petrol driven railcars. Most passengers were going to Murcar Golf Club and when the brickworks closed in 1924 the golf club purchased the line. Services for golfers continued up until 1949 with about six to seven return workings daily, mainly during the summer months.

Old Meldrum – Inverurie (Inverurie Junction)

Passenger service withdrawn	2 November 1931	*Stations closed*	*Date*
Distance	5.25 miles	Old Meldrum	2 November 1931
Company	Great North of Scotland	Fingask Paltform	2 November 1931
		Lethenty	2 November 1931

Old Meldrum Station, 1914.

Opened in 1856, this branch line left the present day Aberdeen to Inverurie line at Inverurie. Initially, the line operated as the Inverurie and Old Meldrum Junction Railway but due to financial difficulties the Great North of Scotland took over the line two years later. At first the line was five and three quarter miles but when a new station at Inverurie was opened in 1902 the distance was reduced by half a mile. Old Meldrum Station was badly situated as it was actually outside the town and this, coupled with the fact that the road journey was easier, resulted in the withdrawal of passenger services in 1931. Freight services lasted until January 1966.

Peterhead – Maud (Maud Junction)

Passenger service withdrawn	3 May 1965	*Stations Closed*	*Date*
Distance	13 miles	Inverugie	3 May 1965
Company	Great North of Scotland	Newseat Halt	3 May 1965
		Longside	3 May 1965
Stations Closed	*Date*	Mintlaw *	3 May 1965
Peterhead	3 May 1965	Abbey of Deer Platform **	After 1937

Peterhead Station, August 1957.

* Known as Old Deer until September 1867.

** The platform used by visitors to the New Deer Abbey.

Inverugie Station, 1951.

Forming part of the Buchan line route, the branch to Peterhead left the Aberdeen to Fraserburgh line at Maud Junction. Although the passenger line terminated at Peterhead Station, the line continued for about another mile to the town's harbour. Fish traffic was the mainstay of the line and although there was a passenger service to Aberdeen it took quite a long time. In 1863 the forty four mile journey took two and three quarter hours, but by 1907 this had been reduced to just under two hours. Travel by road to Peterhead from Aberdeen was fifteen miles shorter than the rail journey so it was inevitable that the railway would eventually close. When bus competition came the London and North Eastern Railway Company was worried – it even offered to buy out the bus operator.

Mintlaw Station, *c.* **1908.**

In its later days the line was host to the ill-fated North British diesel electric locomotives which tended to break down and only lasted a few years in service before being scrapped. These were fitted with snow ploughs and token catchers for the single line working. (A token catcher is a device which allows drivers to pick up at speed a large pouch containing a token which represents the authorisation to proceed into the next clear section of single line railway.) The last freight train ran on 4 September 1970 and the site of Peterhead Station is now taken by a school and a housing estate.

Peterhead Admiralty Station – Stirling Hill

Passenger service withdrawn	1920
Distance	2.5 miles
Company	HM Government

Stations closed	*Date*
Peterhead Admiralty Station	1920
Stirling Hill	1920

This railway was built to transport granite from a quarry on Stirling Hill which was just outside of Peterhead. The granite was quarried by labour from the town's prison and was used by the Admiralty in the construction of a breakwater at Peterhead harbour. Work on the breakwater began in 1884 and the railway was built to transport not just the granite but also the prison force. The line was constructed to a high standard and had its own signalling system. There was a regular passenger service with two trains in each direction daily, carrying about one hundred prisoners and officers.

St Combs – Fraserburgh (Fraserburgh Junction)

Passenger service withdrawn	3 May 1965		
Distance	5.25 miles		
Company	Great North of Scotland		

Stations closed	*Date*
St Combs	3 May 1965
Cairnbulg *	3 May 1965
Philorth Bridge Halt	3 May 1965
Kirkton Bridge Platform **	3 May 1965

St Combs Station.

* Known as Inverallochy until September 1903.

** Known as Kirkton Bridge Halt until June 1908.

The last railway line to be built by the Great North of Scotland was this branch from Fraserburgh to St Combs. Constructed as a light railway under the Light Railways Act of 1896, it opened to passenger traffic on 1 July 1903. The 1922 Bradshaw timetable for the line gave six arrivals and departures on weekdays with some trains carrying both passenger coaches and goods wagons. The five and a quarter mile trip took twenty minutes and there were two halts on the line with trains stopping on request. One of the stipulations of the Light Railways Act was that no train should exceed 25 m.p.h and as the line was unfenced in many areas, each locomotive was fitted with cowcatchers in case strays wandered on to the line. Kirkton Bridge Halt was used mainly by members of Fraserburgh Golf Club and at one time in the London and North Eastern days special funeral trains were run to Philorth Bridge Halt for the nearby cemetery. During the Second World War Cairnbulg Station was used to transport personnel and materials to Fraserburgh airfield which was used by planes coming in from the North Sea. Freight services to St Combs and Cairnbulg were withdrawn in 1960.

Closed passenger stations on lines still open to passenger services

Line/Service	Edinburgh – Aberdeen *	Station	Date of closure
		Ferryhill	2 August 1854

Cairnie Junction, April 1965.

* The closed stations on this line that were in Lothian, Fife, Angus and Kincardineshire were Turnhouse, Donibristle Halt, Sinclairtown, Dysart, Thornton Junction, Falkland Road, Kingskettle, Dairsie, St Fort, Esplanade, Dundee East (first), Craigie, Roodyards, Stannergate, West Ferry, Buddon, Carnoustie (first), Easthaven, Elliot Junction, Letham Grange, Cauldcots, Inverkeilor, Lunan Bay, Hillside, Craigo, Marykirk, Laurencekirk, Fordoun, Drumlithie, Carmont, Muchalls, Newtonhill, Portlethen, Cove Bay and Limpet Hill.

Line/Service	Inverness – Aberdeen *	Station	Date of closure
		Pitmedden	7 December 1964
Station	Date of closure	Dyce (first)	17 July 1861
Cairnie Junction **	6 May 1968	Dyce ***	6 May 1968
Rothiemay	6 May 1968	Stoneywood	5 April 1937
Gartly	6 May 1968	Bankhead	5 April 1937
Kennethmont	6 May 1968	Bucksburn	5 March 1956
Wardhouse	5 June 1961	Persley Halt ****	5 April 1937
Buchanstone	September 1866	Woodside	5 April 1937
Oyne	6 May 1968	Don Street	5 April 1937
Pitcaple	6 May 1968	Kittybrewster (first)	4 November 1867
Inveramsay	1 October 1951	Kittybrewster	6 May 1968
Inverurie (first)	10 February 1902	Hutcheon Street	5 April 1937
Kintore	7 December 1964	Schoolhill	5 April 1937
Kinaldie	7 December 1964		

The bridge at Rothiemay Station, c. 1905.

* The closed stations on this line which were in Inverness-shire, Nairn, Banff and Moray were Allanfearn, Castle Stuart Platform, Dalcross, Gollanfield, Kildrummie, Auldearn, Brodie, Kinloss (first, second and third), Alves, Mosstowie, Lhanbryde, Orbliston, Orton, Mulben, Tauchers Halt and Grange.

** Known as Cairnie Platform until 1919.
*** Reopened 15 September 1984.
**** Known as Persley until 16 July 1926.

Oyne Station, *c.* 1908.

Pitcaple Station.

Two engines at Kittybrewster Station, August 1957. *Above*: a 'Yorkie' tank, built by the Yorkshire Engine Company; *right*: a Manning, Wardle tank which was used for shunting in the dock area.